Piano / Vocal / Guitar

ARETHA FRANKLIN
20 GREATEST HITS

D0743667

Cover photo by David Redfern / Redferns / Getty Images

ISBN 978-1-4803-8459-0

HAL•LEONARD® CORPORATION

7777 W. BLUEMOUND RD. P.O. BOX 13819 MILWAUKEE, WI 53213

Visit Hal Leonard Online at
www.halleonard.com

AIN'T NO WAY

Words and Music by
CAROLYN FRANKLIN

BABY, I LOVE YOU

Words and Music by
RONNIE SHANNON

Some-day, _____ you might want to run a-way _____

and leave _____ me sit-ting here cry-ing.

But if it's all the same _____ to you, ba-by, I'm gon-na

stop you from say-ing good-bye. _____ Ba-by, I

CHAIN OF FOOLS

Words and Music by
DON COVAY

DO RIGHT WOMAN DO RIGHT MAN

Words and Music by DAN PENN
and CHIPS MOMAN

make me do wrong.

Take me for grant - ed; leav - ing

love un - sure makes

will - pow - er weak and

DR. FEELGOOD
(Love Is a Serious Business)

Words and Music by ARETHA FRANKLIN
and TED WHITE

DON'T PLAY THAT SONG
(You Lied)

Words and Music by AHMET ERTEGUN
and BETTY NELSON

Moderately fast Shuffle

Don't __ play that song __ for me __

'cause __ it brings __ back __ mem - o - ries __

THE HOUSE THAT JACK BUILT

Words and Music by BOBBY LANCE
and FRAN ROBINS

Moderate R&B groove

This is the house _ that Jack _ built, _ y'all. _   Re-mem-ber this house. _

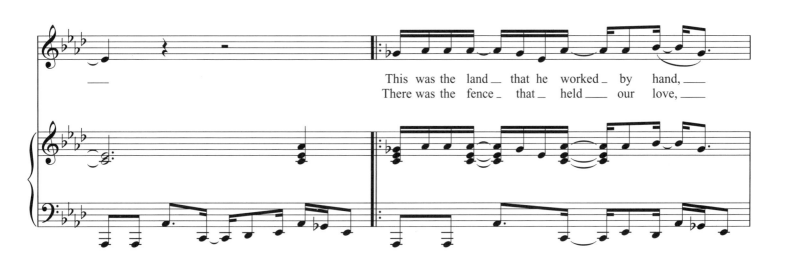

This was the land _ that he worked _ by hand, _
There was the fence _ that _ held _ our love, _

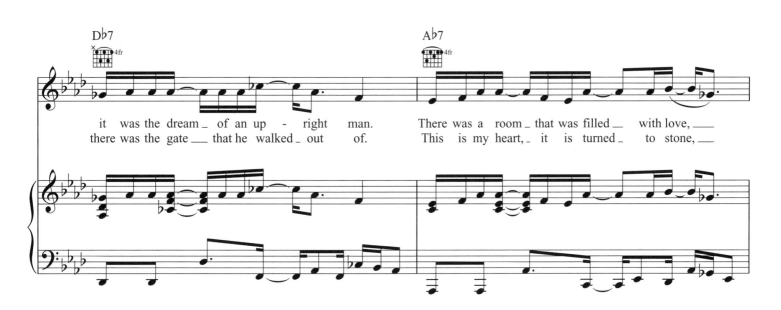

it was the dream _ of an up - right man.   There was a room _ that was filled _ with love, _
there was the gate _ that he walked _ out of.   This is my heart, _ it is turned _ to stone, _

FREEWAY OF LOVE

Words and Music by NARADA MICHAEL WALDEN
and JEFFREY COHEN

Driving Pop Groove

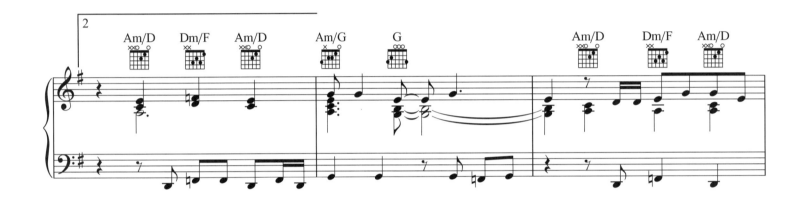

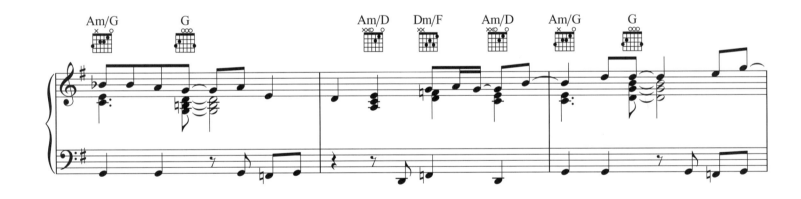

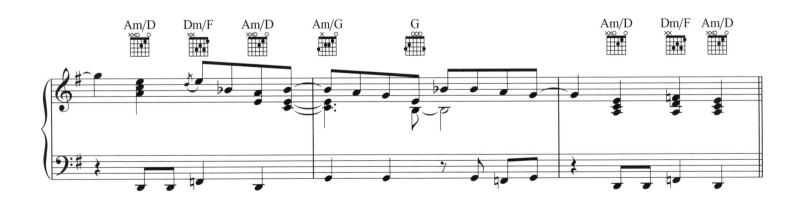

I KNEW YOU WERE WAITING
(For Me)

Words and Music by SIMON CLIMIE
and DENNIS MORGAN

I NEVER LOVED A MAN
(The Way I Love You)

Words and Music by
RONNIE SHANNON

Moderate Blues

You're a no good __ heart __ break- er,

you're a li- ar and you're a cheat. And I don't know why __

I let you do __ these things to me.

I SAY A LITTLE PRAYER

Lyric by HAL DAVID
Music by BURT BACHARACH

Moderately fast

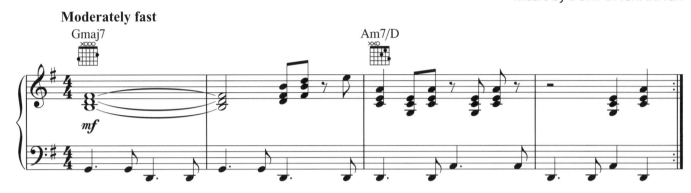

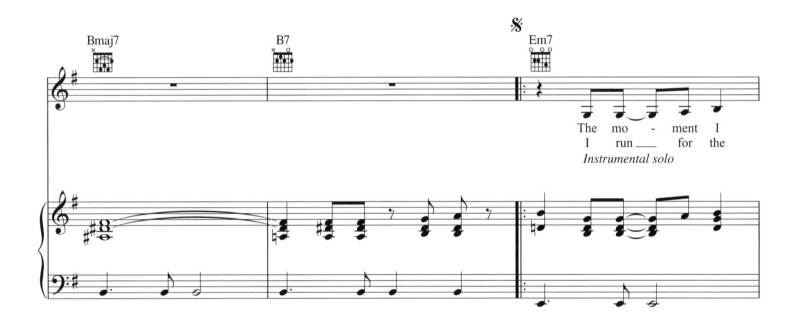

The mo - ment I
I run ___ for the
Instrumental solo

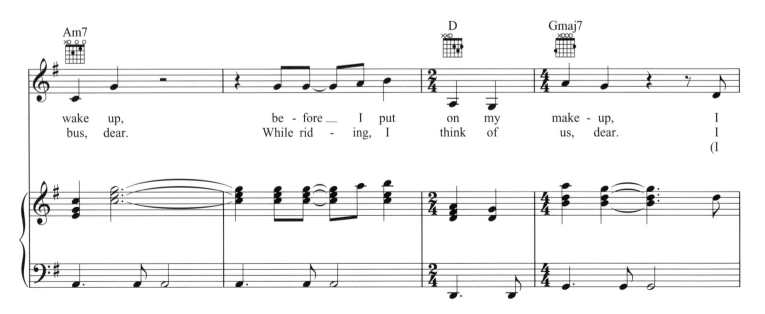

wake up,
bus, dear.

be - fore ___ I put on my make - up,
While rid - ing, I think of us, dear.

I
I
(I

(You Make Me Feel Like)
A NATURAL WOMAN

Words and Music by GERRY GOFFIN,
CAROLE KING and JERRY WEXLER

RESPECT

Words and Music by
OTIS REDDING

Moderately fast

(Ooh)　　What you want,

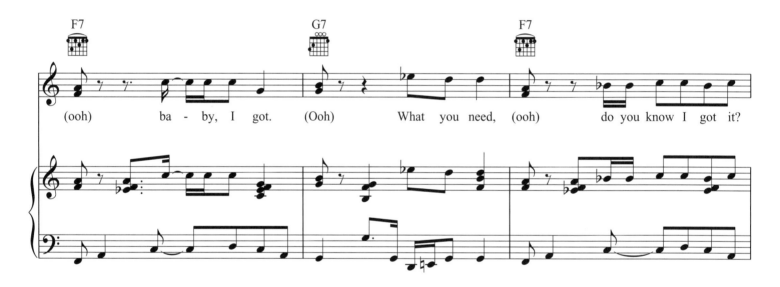

(ooh)　　ba - by, I got. (Ooh)　　What you need, (ooh)　　do you know I got it?

(Ooh)　　All I'm ask - in' (ooh)　　is for a lit-tle re - spect when you come home.　　Hey,
(Just　a　lit - tle　bit,)

ROCK STEADY

Words and Music by
ARETHA FRANKLIN

stead-y, ba-by, that's what I feel now.

Let's call the song exactly what it is.

Step 'n' move your hips with a feel-ing from side to side. ____

Sit your-self down in your car ___ and take a ride. ___ And while you're mov - in'

rock stead-y, rock stead-y, ba - by,

let's call this song ex - act - ly what it is. (What it is, what it is, what it

stead - y,   rock   stead - y, ba - by.   Rock

staed - y,   rock   stead - y, ba - by.

A ROSE IS STILL A ROSE

Words and Music by LAURYN HILL,
EDIE BRICKELL, KENNETH WITHROW,
JOHN BUSH, JOHN HOUSER
and ALAN ALY

Moderately, not too fast

* *Recorded a half step higher.*

SAVE ME

Words and Music by ARETHA FRANKLIN,
CAROLYN FRANKLIN and CURTIS OUSLEY

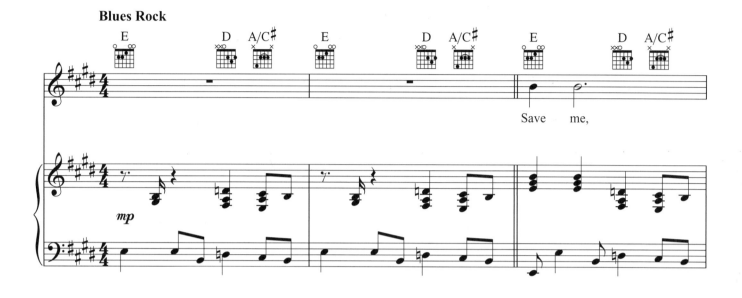

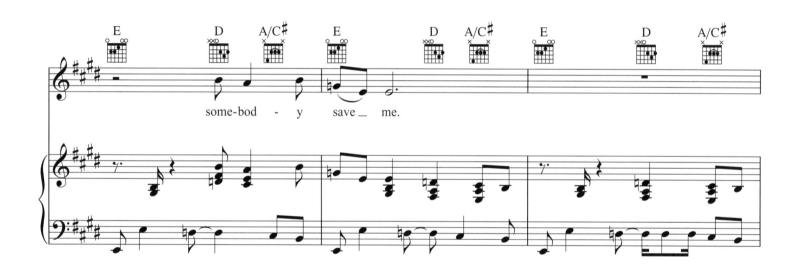

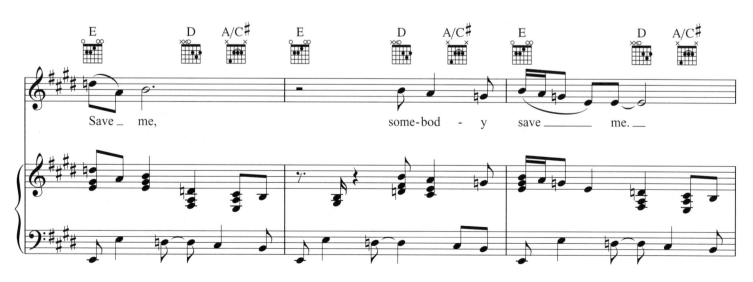

SINCE YOU'VE BEEN GONE
(Sweet, Sweet Baby)

Words and Music by ARETHA FRANKLIN
and TED WHITE

Ba - by, ba - by, sweet ba - by,

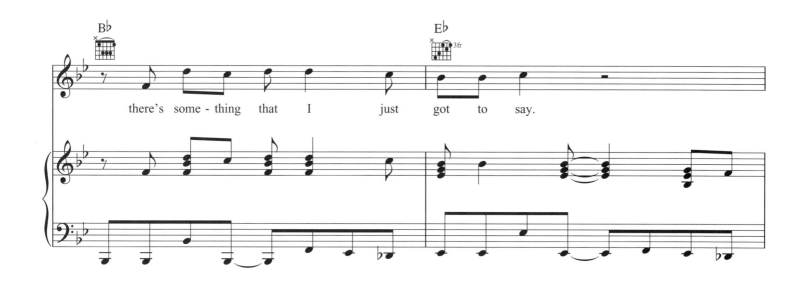

there's some - thing that I just got to say.

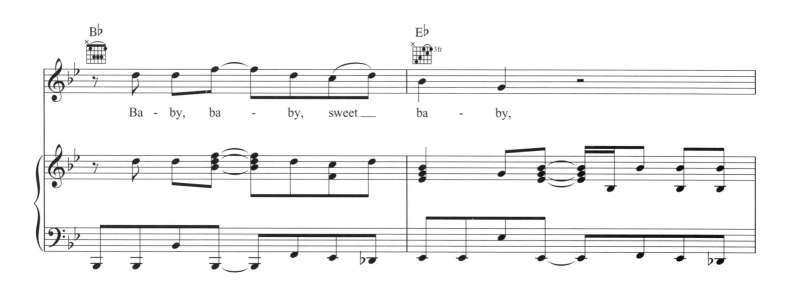

Ba - by, ba - by, sweet _____ ba - by,

SPANISH HARLEM

Words and Music by JERRY LEIBER
and PHIL SPECTOR

THINK

Words and Music by ARETHA FRANKLIN
and TED WHITE

UNTIL YOU COME BACK TO ME
(That's What I'm Gonna Do)

Words and Music by STEVIE WONDER,
MORRIS BROADNAX and CLARENCE O. PAUL

Though you don't call an-y-more,
I sit and wait
in vain.
I guess I'll rap on your door,
tap on your win - dow - pane,

have to de - cide
you had to set
me free?
I'm going to swal-low my pride and
beg you to please, ba - by, please see me.

I'm goin' to